City Mouse and Country Mouse

by Megan Howard
illustrated by David Bergstein

Editorial Offices: Glenview, Illinois • Parsippany, New Jersey • New York, New York
Sales Offices: Needham, Massachusetts • Duluth, Georgia • Glenview, Illinois
Coppell, Texas • Ontario, California • Mesa, Arizona

City Mouse was tired of the city. So one day, she went to see her friend in the country. The mice ate homemade soup. They climbed trees. They picked beautiful flowers. They rolled down hills.

"I like the country. Birds sing and stars shine," said City Mouse. "But it is so quiet!"

"I know," said Country Mouse. "Maybe the city is better."

The very next day Country Mouse went to see her friend in the city. The mice went roller-skating on the sidewalk. They ate bread at a bakery. They saw someone sing at a club.

"See why I missed the city?" said City Mouse.

"I do like the city," said Country
Mouse. "There is a lot to do. But I am
tired. I need some peace and quiet."

"I think I like the country better," said Country Mouse. "But I had fun today."

"Me too," said City Mouse. "You go back to the country. I will stay in the city. Let's meet somewhere and visit again soon."

Country Life and City Life

In the story, Country Mouse and City Mouse live in very different places. Country Mouse can hear birds sing in the country. She has flowers, trees, hills, and open land. City Mouse lives with many people around her in the city. She can do fun things like roller-skating or shopping or going to a club. Each mouse visits the other place. Each mouse learns that she likes her own place better.

Many people live in the country. Many other people live in the city. Both places are special in their own ways.